TABLE OF CONTENTS

THE MIRACLE CATCH

Lerner **SPORTS**

SUPER SPORTS
TEAMS

INSIDE THE
NEW YORK
GIANTS

CHRISTINA HILL

Lerner Publications ◆ Minneapolis

SPORTS THRILLS
MEET
RESEARCH SKILLS

Lerner SPORTS

Free Database Trial: **lernersports.com**

Lerner Publications Company
An imprint of Lerner Publishing Group, Inc.
241 First Avenue North
Minneapolis, MN 55401 USA

For reading levels and more information, look up this title at www.lernerbooks.com.

Main body text set in Aptifer Slab LT Pro / Typeface provided by Linotype AG

Library of Congress Cataloging-in-Publication Data

Title: Inside the New York Giants / Christina Hill.
Description: Minneapolis : Lerner Publications, 2023. | Series: Super sports teams (Lerner sports) | Includes bibliographical references and index. | Audience: Ages 7–11 | Audience: Grades 2–3 | Summary: "The New York Giants have played football for almost one hundred years. Explore the team's long history, epic moments, most legendary players, and much more"— Provided by publisher.
Identifiers: LCCN 2021057408 (print) | LCCN 2021057409 (ebook) | ISBN 9781728458090 (library binding) | ISBN 9781728463421 (paperback) | ISBN 9781728462370 (ebook)
Subjects: LCSH: New York Giants (Football team)—History—Juvenile literature.
Classification: LCC GV956.N4 H55 2023 (print) | LCC GV956.N4 (ebook) | DDC 796.332/64097471—dc23

LC record available at https://lccn.loc.gov/2021057408
LC ebook record available at https://lccn.loc.gov/2021057409

Manufactured in the United States of America
1 – CG – 7/15/22

FACTS AT A GLANCE

- The **GIANTS** have won the Super Bowl four times: 1987, 1991, 2008, and 2012.

- Fans often call the Giants the **G-MEN** or **BIG BLUE**.

- Linebacker **LAWRENCE TAYLOR** is one of the greatest National Football League (NFL) players of all time.

- The New York Giants play their home games in **NEW JERSEY**.

- The **OFFICIAL TEAM NAME** is the New York Football Giants.

Football fans consider the 2008 Super Bowl to be one of the greatest Super Bowls of all time. The NFL ranks it as the fifth greatest game in the league's history. The New York Giants faced the New England Patriots. The Patriots entered the game with a perfect regular season record.

The game remained close in the fourth quarter, but the Giants were trailing 14–10. In the final two minutes of the game, Giants quarterback Eli Manning tried to find an opening as the New England defense charged toward him. With a cluster of Patriots surrounding Manning, it appeared to be over for the Giants. But Manning broke free. He looked down the field. He had only a few seconds to throw the ball. Manning spotted wide receiver David Tyree. Manning launched the ball down the middle of the field.

Tyree saw the ball coming his way, but so did Patriots defender Rodney Harrison. The two players jumped into the air at the same time. Tyree managed to secure the football with one hand by pressing it against his helmet. As he fell to the ground, he grabbed the ball tightly with both hands. Fans cheered at Tyree's miracle "helmet catch." The Giants went on to score and won the game 17–14.

David Tyree leaps and presses the ball against his helmet.

Tyree celebrates with teammates during the 2008 Super Bowl. He played for the Giants for five seasons.

Linebackers Harry Carson (*left*) and Gary Reasons (*right*) were key players in the Big Blue Wrecking Crew defense during the 1980s.

THE G-MEN

New York City businessperson Tim Mara started the New York Football Giants in 1925. He borrowed the name from a Major League Baseball (MLB) team called the New York Giants. He added the word *Football* to set the two teams apart. *Giants* is a reference to the tall skyscrapers in New York City. The team is still owned by Tim Mara's grandson, John Mara, and Steve Tisch.

Co-owners John Mara (*left*) and Steve Tisch (*right*) have won two Super Bowls with the Giants.

The team is still officially the New York Football Giants, but most fans know them as the Giants or the G-Men. Fans also call the team Big Blue because of their blue helmets. In the 1980s, their tough defense earned the nicknames the Big Blue Wrecking Crew and the Crunch Bunch.

Lawrence Taylor (*center*) and the Big Blue Wrecking Crew were one of the greatest NFL defenses of all time.

The Giants played one season at Shea Stadium. The building was torn down in 2009.

The Giants have had many homes. From 1925 to 1955, the Giants played at the Polo Grounds in New York City. In 1956, they started playing in Yankee Stadium, home of MLB's New York Yankees. But when that stadium had to be repaired in 1973, the team had no home. They played at the Yale Bowl at Yale University in Connecticut in 1973 and 1974. They played at Shea Stadium in 1975, the home of the New York Mets baseball team.

The team played in Giants Stadium for 33 years.

Finally, in 1976, the Giants moved into Giants Stadium. Eight years later, the New York Jets, another NFL team, needed a place to play. So they moved into Giants Stadium too. Early in the 21st century, the teams decided to build and share a more modern and updated stadium. They partnered to build MetLife Stadium in New Jersey, which opened in 2010.

MetLife is one of only two stadiums in the NFL that is shared by two teams.

Eli Manning holds the Vince Lombardi Trophy in 2012 after winning the Super Bowl.

AMAZING MOMENTS

The New York Giants have had many years of football excellence. In 1927, the Giants won their first NFL Championship. In 1966, the NFL merged with the American Football League (AFL). After the two leagues joined, the NFL Championship became the Super Bowl.

Offensive line star Steve Owen was the captain of the 1927 team and helped lead the Giants to victory that year. In 1930, he became their head coach. He remained in charge for 24 seasons. Under his leadership, the Giants had some of their most amazing moments.

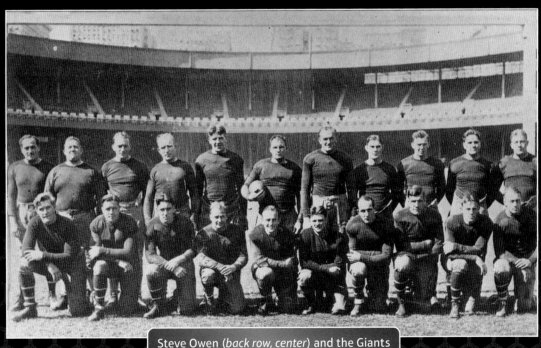

Steve Owen (*back row, center*) and the Giants lost only one game during the 1927 season.

In 1934, the Giants faced the Chicago Bears in the NFL Championship at the Polo Grounds. Freezing rain fell the night before and froze the ground. Despite wearing cleats, players on both teams struggled to stop sliding on the field.

At halftime, the Bears were winning 10–3. But Coach Owen had a plan. One of his players suggested that they might play better on the frozen field in regular shoes. He thought the flat rubber surface of the shoes would be less slippery than the rounded bumps on their cleats. So Owen borrowed basketball shoes from a nearby college and had his players change into them during halftime. This smart move gave the Giants the sure footing they needed. They dominated the second half of the game. The Giants scored four touchdowns in the fourth quarter and won 30–13.

Phil Simms won the Super Bowl Most Valuable Player award in 1987 for completing 22 passes for 268 yards and three touchdowns.

The Giants won their first Super Bowl in 1987 against the Denver Broncos. Led by quarterback Phil Simms and the Big Blue Wrecking Crew defense, the Giants scored 30 points in the second half of the game. They defeated the Broncos 39–20.

The Giants returned to the Super Bowl again in 1991. They played the Buffalo Bills. The game was close from start to finish. With only eight seconds left, the Bills missed a field goal, and the Giants won by a single point, 20–19. Giants running back Ottis Anderson was named Most Valuable Player (MVP) of the game. He had 102 rushing yards, including one touchdown.

The Giants defeated the Patriots in the 2008 Super Bowl. They faced each other again in the 2012 Super Bowl. The Giants started off strong with a 9–0 lead in the first quarter, but then the Patriots pulled ahead. By the third quarter, the Giants were trailing by eight points. They kicked two field goals to make the score 17–15. Then, with 57 seconds left, running back Ahman Bradshaw scored a touchdown. The Giants won 21–17. Eli Manning won the Super Bowl MVP award for the second time. He completed 30 of 40 passes for 296 yards, one touchdown, and no interceptions.

The 1991 Super Bowl ranks 10th on the NFL's list of greatest games.

Phil Simms led the Giants to victory in the 1987 Super Bowl. Four years later, he injured his foot during the season and was unable to play in the 1991 Super Bowl.

GIANTS SUPERSTARS

The Giants have a history full of superstars, but a few key players and coaches top the charts. Bill Parcells took the job of Giants head coach in 1983. He coached the team for eight seasons and led them to two of their Super Bowl wins. Under his leadership, the Giants had some of their best seasons.

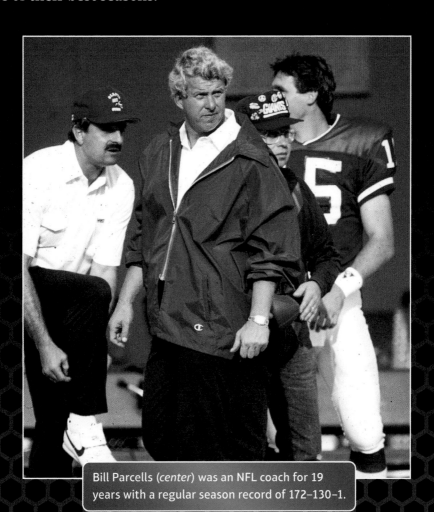

Bill Parcells (*center*) was an NFL coach for 19 years with a regular season record of 172–130–1.

Quarterback Phil Simms spent his entire NFL career with the Giants from 1979 to 1993. Simms won the Super Bowl MVP award in 1987 for his performance against the Broncos. He completed 22 of 25 passes in that game. Simms ended his playing career with 199 touchdown passes. After retiring from playing, Simms began a career as a football broadcaster on TV.

Many fans think of linebacker Lawrence Taylor as the greatest Giants player of all time. He played for the team from 1981 to 1993. He was part of the famous Crunch Bunch defense. Taylor led the Giants to two Super Bowl victories and earned NFL Defensive Player of the Year three times. During his NFL career, he had 132.5 official sacks and nine interceptions.

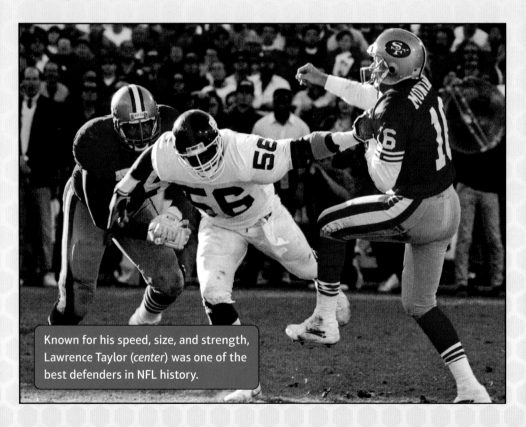

Known for his speed, size, and strength, Lawrence Taylor (*center*) was one of the best defenders in NFL history.

Tiki Barber played for the Giants in all 10 seasons of his NFL career.

Running back Tiki Barber played for the Giants for his entire NFL career, from 1997 to 2006. He tops the Giants charts with 10,449 career rushing yards. Coaches, players, and fans voted for Barber to play in three Pro Bowls.

Quarterback Eli Manning joined the Giants in 2004 and played for the team until 2019. Manning comes from a football family. His dad, Archie, and brother, Peyton, were also NFL quarterbacks. Despite a shaky start as a rookie, Manning pulled through and led the Giants to two Super Bowl wins.

Many fans consider this play by Odell Beckham Jr. to be the best catch in Giants history—and maybe the best in NFL history too.

The Giants drafted wide receiver Odell Beckham Jr. in 2014. During his rookie year, he made a famous one-handed touchdown catch against the Dallas Cowboys. Beckham went on to win Offensive Rookie of the Year that season.

Saquon Barkley was a first-round draft pick in 2018 and won the Offensive Rookie of the Year award for his superstar first season. Barkley led the NFL with 2,028 combined rushing and receiving yards. He also ranked number 16 on the NFL Top 100 Players of 2019.

Saquon Barkley is a great athlete who also excelled in basketball and track and field in high school.

Giants fans show up to cheer for their team, rain or shine.

GO, BIG BLUE!

Giants fans fill the stands at MetLife Stadium, one of the largest stadiums in the NFL. It seats 82,500 fans and has a video screen in every corner. No fan misses a single second of the action! Giants fans cheer "Go, Big Blue!" to support their favorite team. The Giants wear red, white, and blue uniforms, but their helmets are always blue.

Giants helmets have changed over the years, but they've always been blue.

The Giants have not returned to the Super Bowl since their big win in 2012. But they are building a team of new superstars to take them there. Running back Saquon Barkley missed most of the 2020 season due to an injury, but fans are happy to see him back on the field. The Giants drafted quarterback Daniel Jones in 2019. He had a great rookie season. Fans are confident he will lead the Giants to many future wins.

The Giants are one of the NFL's most successful teams. New York fans are looking forward to a bright future. They hope Big Blue will dominate the NFL once again.

Giants players dance to celebrate a touchdown in 2021.

Quarterback Daniel Jones was the sixth pick in the 2019 NFL Draft.

GIANTS
SEASON RECORD HOLDERS

RUSHING TOUCHDOWNS

1. Joe Morris, 21 (1985)
2. Brandon Jacobs, 15 (2008)
3. Joe Morris, 14 (1986)
   Ottis Anderson, 14 (1989)
   Rodney Hampton, 14 (1992)

RECEIVING TOUCHDOWNS

1. Homer Jones, 13 (1967)
   Odell Beckham Jr., 13 (2015)
2. Del Shofner, 12 (1962)
   Plaxico Burress, 12 (2007)
   Odell Beckham Jr., 12 (2014)

PASSING YARDS

1. Eli Manning, 4,933 (2011)
2. Eli Manning, 4,432 (2015)
3. Eli Manning, 4,410 (2014)
4. Eli Manning, 4,299 (2018)
5. Kerry Collins, 4,073 (2002)

RUSHING YARDS

1. Tiki Barber, 1,860 (2005)
2. Tiki Barber, 1,662 (2006)
3. Tiki Barber, 1,518 (2004)
4. Joe Morris, 1,516 (1986)
5. Tiki Barber, 1,387 (2002)

PASS CATCHES

1. Steve Smith, 107 (2009)
2. Odell Beckham Jr., 101 (2016)
3. Odell Beckham Jr., 96 (2015)
4. Odell Beckham Jr., 91 (2014)
   Saquon Barkley, 91 (2018)

SACKS

1. Michael Strahan, 22.5 (2001)
2. Lawrence Taylor, 20.5 (1986)
3. Michael Strahan, 18.5 (2003)
4. Jason Pierre-Paul, 16.5 (2011)
5. Leonard Marshall, 15.5 (1985)

GLOSSARY

broadcaster: a person who speaks during a sports event on TV

cleat: a shoe with plastic or metal spikes or wedges on the bottom to prevent slipping

draft: when teams take turns choosing new players

field goal: a score of three points in football made by kicking the ball over the crossbar

franchise: a team that is a member of a professional sports league

interception: a pass caught by the defending team that results in a change of possession

linebacker: a defender who usually plays in the middle of the defense

offensive line: the five players on the offensive side of the line of scrimmage who block defenders

Pro Bowl: the NFL's all-star game

rookie: a first-year player

sack: to tackle the quarterback behind the line of scrimmage

LEARN MORE

Fishman, Jon M. *Saquon Barkley*. Minneapolis: Lerner Publications, 2020.

The New York Giants
https://www.giants.com

New York Giants Hall of Famers
https://www.profootballhof.com/teams/new-york-giants/

Osborne, M. K. *Superstars of the New York Giants*. Mankato, MN: Amicus, 2019.

Scheff, Matt. *The Super Bowl: Football's Game of the Year*. Minneapolis: Lerner Publications, 2021.

Sports Illustrated Kids—Football
https://www.sikids.com/football

INDEX

PHOTO ACKNOWLEDGMENTS

Image credits: Donald Miralle/Stringer/Getty Images, p. 4; Rhona Wise/Icon SMI/Newscom, p. 6; Karl Mondon/MCT/Newscom, p. 7; Chuck Solomon/Icon SMI/Newscom, p. 8; Rob Carr/Staff/Getty Images, p. 9; Sporting News Archives/Icon SMI/Newscom, p. 10; George Garrigues/Wikimedia, p. 11; Liftarn/Wikimedia, p. 12; Sarah Stier/Stringer/Getty Images, p. 13; Rob Carr/Staff/Getty Images, p. 14; Pro Football Hall of Fame/Associated Press, p. 15; George Rose/Stringer/Getty Images, p. 16; George Rose/Stringer/Getty Images, p. 17; Mike Powell/Staff/Getty Images, p. 18; SportsChrome/Newscom, p. 19; Al Golub/ZUMA Press/Newscom, p. 20; Jamie Squire/Staff/Getty Images, p. 21; Al Bello/Staff/Getty Images, p. 22; Sarah Stier/Staff/Getty Images, p. 23; Elsa/Staff/Getty Images, p. 24; Rob Carr/Staff/Getty Images, p. 25; Julio Aguilar/Stringer/Getty Images, p. 26; Al Bello/Staff/Getty Images, p. 27; Brian Killian/Stringer/Getty Images, p. 28

Design element: Master3D/Shutterstock.com.

Cover image: Al Bello/Staff/Getty Images